Wolfgang Halm   Geoffrey P. Burwell

Sätze aus dem Alltagsgespräch

deutsch–englisch

Phrases from
Everyday Conversation

German–English

W0245677

MAX HUEBER VERLAG

ISBN 3–19–00.2109–0

4. Auflage 1974

© 1968 Max Hueber Verlag München

Umschlaggestaltung: Wolfgang A. Taube, München

Gesamtherstellung: Druckerei G. J. Manz AG, Dillingen/Donau

Printed in Germany

Lieber Leser,

wenn Sie dieses Büchlein schon gekauft haben, dann wissen Sie wohl warum, und ich brauche Ihnen nicht mehr zu sagen, wofür es gut ist. Wenn Sie aber erst zweifelnd in der Buchhandlung stehen und überlegen, ob Ihnen das Ding die paar Mark wert ist, kann ich Ihnen ein bißchen helfen.

In einer ganz normalen, alltäglichen Unterhaltung in der Fremdsprache – ganz gleich, ob Sie Anfänger oder Fortgeschrittener sind oder nach längerer Unterbrechung wieder einmal ins Ausland fahren – spüren Sie selbst und die andern auch, daß Sie sich nicht ganz „normal" ausdrücken, daß Ihnen für bestimmte einfache Situationen der richtige Satz fehlt, daß es vielleicht sogar zu Mißverständnissen kommt... Stecken Sie das Büchlein in die Tasche, lesen sie öfters mal hier zehn Sätze, dort zehn Sätze, und Sie werden sehen, wie Sie sich bald bei Ihren einfachen Gesprächen und beim Schreiben von Privatbriefen leichter tun.

Sind Sie aber Lehrer (wie ich), dann schlage ich Ihnen vor, Ihren Schülern das Büchlein zur Vorbereitung von kleinen Gesprächs-, Brief- und Aufsatzübungen zu empfehlen. Aus solchen Übungen heraus ist nämlich das Büchlein entstanden. Es kann das Auftreten „typischer Fehler" von vornherein etwas einschränken und damit die Stunde für Lehrer und Schüler noch angenehmer und gewinnbringender werden lassen. Alle Sätze sind *in beiden Sprachen* idiomatisch so richtig, daß das Büchlein zum Englischlernen ebenso gut verwendet werden kann wie zum Deutschlernen.

Daß in einem solchen Buch Preise, Maße und Gewichte nicht genau, sondern nur mit ungefähren Entsprechungen umgerechnet worden sind, versteht sich von selbst. Daher wird 1 yard mit 1 Meter gleichgestellt (1 yard = 0,9143992 Meter), 1 gallon wird mit 4½ Liter angegeben (1 gallon = 4,5459 Liter) und 10 neue pence bedeuten DM 1,–.

Wolfgang Halm

Dear Reader,

If you have already bought this little book, you have done so for a reason, and there is no need for me to tell you what it can be used for. But if you are standing in the bookshop and wondering whether it is worth the price of a few marks or shillings, I can be of some help to you.

In quite an ordinary, everyday conversation in a foreign language—no matter whether you are a beginner or an advanced student or are going abroad again after a considerable lapse of time—you will notice, and others too, that you can't express yourself quite "normally", that you lack the right sentence for certain simple situations, that misunderstandings may even arise... Put this little book in your pocket, read ten sentences on this page every now and then, ten sentences on that page, and you will soon begin to find that things come more easily in your simple conversations and private letters.

If you are a teacher (as I am), then I suggest you recommend this book to your pupils for preparing short practice exercises in conversation, letter writing and essay writing, for it is from exercises of this kind that this book has come into being. It can help to cut down the number of typical "mistakes" from the outset, thus making the lesson more pleasant and profitable for teacher and pupil alike. All the sentences *in both languages* are idiomatically correct, so that the book can be used equally well for learning German or English.

It is, of course, quite obvious that in a book of this kind the prices, weights and measures have not been worked out exactly, but the rough equivalents, current in the particular language, have been employed; thus 1 yard is used for 1 metre (1 yard = 0.9143992 metre), 1 gallon for $4^1/_2$ litres (1 gallon = 4.5459 litres), 10 new pence (10p) for 1 mark.

Wolfgang Halm

Inhaltsverzeichnis

Table of Contents

Gruß, Begrüßung

1 Guten Morgen.
2 Guten Tag.

3 Guten Abend.
4 Gute Nacht.
5 Wie geht's?
6 Danke.
7 Danke, es geht.
8 Danke, gut.
9 Und Ihnen?
10 Bis nachher.
11 Bis morgen.
12 Alles Gute!
13 Gute Fahrt!
14 Viel Vergnügen!

Greetings

1 Good morning.
2 Good morning. Good afternoon.

3 Good evening. Good night.
4 Good night.
5 How are you?
6 All right, thank you.
7 All right, thank you.
8 Very well, thank you.
9 And how are you?
10 See you later.
11 See you tomorrow.
12 All the best.
13 Have a good journey/trip.
14 Have fun. Enjoy yourself.

Kurzsätze

1 Nein, danke.
2 Bitte.
3 Ja, bitte.
4 Danke. Vielen Dank!

5 Bitte.
6 Verzeihung! Entschuldigen Sie!
7 Wie bitte?
8 Aha. Ich verstehe.
9 Richtig. Stimmt.
10 Natürlich. Klar.
11 Einverstanden.
12 In Ordnung.
13 Eben!
14 Na also!
15 Na endlich!

Phrases

1 No, thanks.
2 Please.
3 Yes, please.
4 Thanks. Thank you. Thank you very much.

5 Not at all. It was a pleasure.
6 I'm sorry. Excuse me.
7 Pardon?
8 Oh, I see.
9 Right. That's right.
10 Of course. I understand.
11 Agreed.
12 All right.
13 Quite.
14 There you are. You see.
15 At last.

16	Fein.	16	Fine. Good.
17	Gern.	17	Certainly.
18	Na ja ...	18	Well, yes.
19	Ach so ...!	19	Oh, I see ...
20	Eigentlich nicht.	20	Not really.
21	Eigentlich schon.	21	Actually, it is (does, etc.).
22	Ungern.	22	I'd rather not.
23	Wenn es sein muß.	23	If you insist.
24	So ungefähr.	24	More or less.
25	Nein, nicht ganz so.	25	No, not quite like that.
26	Hoffentlich.	26	(I) hope so.
27	Hoffentlich nicht.	27	(I) hope not.
28	Keine Sorge!	28	Don't worry.
29	Ach wie dumm!	29	Oh, how silly.
30	Macht nichts.	30	Doesn't matter.
31	Leider. Es tut mir leid.	31	Unfortunately. I'm sorry.
32	Schade!	32	Pity.
33	Nichts zu ändern!	33	Can't be helped.
34	Abgesehen davon!	34	Apart from that.
35	Keine Spur!	35	Not a bit of it.
36	Und ob!	36	And how!
37	Und wenn schon!	37	What of it?
38	Na, und?	38	What about it? So what?
39	Was geht das mich an?	39	What's that got to do with me?

Hinweise

			Directions
1	Achtung! Vorsicht!	1	Mind! Be careful. Look out!
2	Ziehen!	2	Pull.
3	Drücken!	3	Push.
4	Frisch gestrichen.	4	Wet paint.
5	Rauchen verboten.	5	No smoking.
6	Eingang.	6	Entrance.
7	Ausgang.	7	Exit.
8	Einwurf DM 1,– (sprich: eine Mark).	8	Insert 10p (tenpence).

Sätze für 1000 Gespräche

1 Ich bin sicher.
2 Ich nehme es an.
3 Ich bin nicht ganz sicher.
4 Ich weiß es nicht.
5 Woher soll ich denn das wissen?
6 Keine Ahnung.
7 Ich verstehe schon.
8 Ich kann mir das gut vorstellen.
9 Ich erinnere mich. Ich erinnere mich daran.
10 Ich denke ja. Ich glaube schon.
11 Ich glaube nicht.
12 Das will ich nicht sagen!
13 Das habe ich nicht gesagt!
14 Ich meinte etwas anderes.
15 Abwarten! Mal abwarten.
16 Mal sehen.
17 Wenn Sie wollen.
18 Wie Sie wollen.
19 Wann Sie wollen.
20 Wie es Ihnen am besten paßt.
21 Es macht mir gar nichts aus.
22 Ich habe nichts dagegen.
23 Ich hätte nichts dagegen.
24 Ich denke dran. Ich vergesse es nicht.
25 Ich muß es mir noch überlegen.
26 Sie können sich's ja überlegen.
27 Ich mache mich gleich dran.

Sentences for 1,000 conversations

1 I'm certain.
2 I suppose so.
3 I'm not quite sure.
4 I don't know.
5 How am I expected to know that?
6 No idea.
7 Oh, I see.
8 I can well imagine that.
9 I remember. I remember that.
10 I think so.
11 I don't think so.
12 I wouldn't say that.
13 I didn't say that.
14 I meant something else.
15 Wait for it. Wait and see.
16 We'll have to wait and see.
17 If you want.
18 As you wish.
19 When you want.
20 As it suits you.
21 It doesn't matter to me at all.
22 I don't mind.
23 I wouldn't mind.
24 I'll remember. I won't forget. I'll bear it in mind.
25 I'll have to think about it.
26 You can think about it.
27 I'll get on with it straight away.

28 Sie können sich darauf verlassen.	28 You can rely on it.
29 Ich verlasse mich darauf!	29 I'm relying on it.
30 Mal sehen, was sich machen läßt.	30 Have to see what can be done.
31 Das muß sich erst zeigen. Das wird sich zeigen.	31 That remains to be seen.
32 Man kann noch nichts sagen.	32 It's not yet possible to say.
33 Vielleicht ist es gar nicht mehr nötig.	33 Perhaps it's no longer necessary.
34 Ich werde mich mal danach erkundigen.	34 I'll ask about it.
35 Ich wollte nur mal fragen.	35 I only wanted to ask.
36 Ich wüßte es gern. Ich hätte es gern gewußt.	36 I should like to know. I should have liked to have known.
37 Ich dachte nur ...	37 I was only thinking ...
38 Ich glaube nicht, daß ich mich täusche/irre.	38 I don't think I'm mistaken.
39 Vielleicht verwechseln Sie es mit etwas anderem.	39 Perhaps you're getting it mixed up with something else.
40 Ich habe das mit etwas anderem verwechselt.	40 I was getting that mixed up with something else.
41 Das kommt vor. Das kann passieren.	41 That does happen. That can happen.
42 Das kann schon sein.	42 That may well be.
43 Was ist schon dabei!	43 What's wrong with that? (There's nothing to it).
44 Was haben Sie davon? Das hat keinen Sinn.	44 What do you get out of it? There's no point in it.
45 Es wäre natürlich schön!	45 It would be very nice, of course.
46 Das kommt aufs gleiche heraus.	46 That amounts to the same thing.
47 Eben!	47 Quite.
48 Das sage ich ja die ganze Zeit!	48 That's what I've been saying all the time.

49 Das habe ich schon immer gesagt!	49 That's what I've always said.
50 Sie werden noch an mich denken!	50 One day you'll believe me.

Positive Meinung
(vgl. Personenbeschreibung S. 23)

Positive Opinion
(cf. Descriptions of People, p. 23)

1 Das Armband ist hübsch.	1 That bracelet is pretty.
2 Es gefällt mir gut.	2 I like it.
3 Ich finde es sehr schön.	3 I think it is very nice.
4 Ich finde es reizend.	4 I think it is charming.
5 Ich mag es furchtbar gern.	5 I like it terribly.
6 Ich liebe diese Dinge.	6 I love this sort of thing.
7 Er hat ganz recht.	7 He's quite right.
8 Das hat er gut gemacht. Das hat er richtig gemacht.	8 He's made a good job of it. He's done it quite right.
9 Er hätte nichts Besseres tun können.	9 He couldn't have done anything better.
10 Ich kann ihn gut verstehen.	10 I can understand him well.
11 Ich kann das sehr gut verstehen.	11 I can understand that very well.

Negative Meinung
(vgl. Personenbeschreibung S. 23)

Negative Opinion
(cf. Descriptions of People, p. 23)

1 Das Armband ist häßlich.	1 That bracelet isn't pretty.
2 Es ist nichts wert.	2 It's not worth anything.
3 Ich finde nichts dran.	3 I can't see anything in it.
4 Es gibt viel hübschere Dinge.	4 There are much prettier things.
5 Ich kann nichts damit anfangen.	5 I can't do anything with it.
6 So etwas Dummes!	6 What a stupid thing!
7 Wie kann er das nur tun! Wie kann er nur so was machen!	7 How can he do such a thing?
8 Das hätte er nicht tun sollen!	8 He shouldn't have done that.

9	Das war ein großer Fehler von ihm!	9	That was a big mistake he made.
10	Der weiß ja gar nicht, was er tut!	10	He has no idea what he's up to.
11	Ich hätte das an seiner Stelle nie gemacht!	11	I would never have done that in his position.
12	Das hat er sich nicht richtig überlegt.	12	He didn't think the matter over properly.

Ausdruck der Zufriedenheit

1 Wie geht's? Wie geht es Ihnen?
2 Ausgezeichnet. Es geht mir ausgezeichnet.
3 Ich kann wirklich nicht klagen.
4 Wir sind alle gesund, was will man mehr?
5 Es geht vorwärts mit der Arbeit.
6 Die Arbeit macht mir Spaß.
7 Bis jetzt geht alles recht gut.
8 Ich habe schon eine ganze Menge erreicht.

Expression of Satisfaction

1 How are things? How are you?
2 Excellent. I feel wonderful.
3 I really can't complain.
4 We're all well, what more can you want?
5 I'm getting on with my work.
6 I enjoy my work.
7 So far everything's gone very well.
8 I've already achieved quite a lot.

Unzufriedenheit, unerfüllte Wünsche

1 Wie geht's? Wie geht es Ihnen?
2 Es geht. Es könnte besser gehen.
3 Ich weiß nicht, was mit mir los ist.
4 Ich bin deprimiert.
5 Ich fühle mich gar nicht wohl.

Dissatisfaction, Unfulfilled Wishes

1 How are things? How are you?
2 Not bad. Could be better.
3 I don't know what's the matter with me.
4 I'm depressed.
5 I don't feel well at all.

6	In letzter Zeit geht alles schief.	6	Everything's gone wrong recently.
7	Ich bringe nichts fertig.	7	I never get anything done.
8	Ich habe zuviel Arbeit. Ich bin überarbeitet.	8	I've got too much work. I'm overworked.
9	Ich habe Ärger mit dem Chef.	9	I'm having trouble with my boss.
10	Es kommt immer alles auf einmal!	10	Everything seems to come at once. It never rains but it pours.
11	Wenn ich nicht alles selbst machen müßte!	11	If only I didn't have to do everything myself.
12	Wenn ich wenigstens mehr Zeit für meine Familie hätte!	12	If only I had more time for my family.
13	Wenn das dumme Geld nicht wäre!	13	If it weren't for money!
14	Ich sitze ziemlich in der Klemme.	14	I'm in quite a fix.

Reihenfolge

Sequence of Events

1	Zuerst gehe ich einkaufen.	1	First I'm going shopping.
2	Dann gehe ich in die Stadt.	2	Then I'm going to town.
3	Anschließend esse ich zusammen mit meiner Freundin.	3	Afterwards I'm eating with my girl friend.
4	Nachher gehen wir vielleicht ins Kino.	4	After that perhaps we'll go to the cinema.
5	Später trinken wir bei mir Tee.	5	Later we'll have tea at my place.
6	Am Anfang wollte ich ihr nichts von meinen Plänen sagen.	6	At first I didn't want to tell her anything about my plans.
7	Am Schluß habe ich es ihr doch gesagt.	7	In the end I did tell her, after all.
8	Das Wichtigste ist die Gesundheit.	8	The most important thing is good health.

9 Vor allem mußt du an deine Familie denken!

9 You have to think of your family first.

Vergleiche

1 Sein Haus ist so groß wie unseres.
2 Es ist sogar etwas größer als das unsere.
3 Es ist nicht so klein wie deines.
4 Es ist viel hübscher, als ich gedacht hatte.
5 Sein Bruder ist viel älter als er.
6 Er ist ein kleines bißchen größer als sein Bruder.
7 Er ist nicht ganz so groß wie du.
8 Er ist bei weitem nicht so groß wie dein Bruder.

Comparisons

1 His house is as large as ours.
2 It is even a little larger than ours.
3 It is not so small as yours.
4 It is much prettier than I thought.
5 His brother is much older than him.
6 He is a little taller than his brother.
7 He is not quite so tall as you.
8 He is by no means so tall as your brother.

Grade

1 Die Prüfung war unheimlich schwierig / enorm schwierig / außerordentlich schwierig
2 sehr schwierig
3 recht schwierig
4 schwierig
5 ziemlich schwierig / gar nicht so leicht
6 gar nicht so schwierig / ziemlich leicht
7 leicht
8 recht leicht
9 ganz leicht

Degrees

1 The exam(ination) was extremely difficult/terribly difficult/extraordinarily difficult
2 very difficult
3 quite difficult
4 difficult
5 rather difficult/not at all easy
6 not at all difficult/fairly easy
7 easy
8 rather easy
9 quite easy

10 sehr leicht	10 very easy
11 kinderleicht	11 dead easy
12 wirklich kinderleicht	12 as easy as pie

Mengen

1 Wieviel?
2 Ich trinke eine Tasse Kaffee,
3 eine Flasche Wein,
4 ein Glas Wasser,
5 einen Kognak, einen doppelten Whisky.
6 Ich esse ein Brot, eine Scheibe Brot,
7 eine Tafel, ein Stückchen Schokolade,
8 einen halben Apfel,
9 ein paar Scheiben Wurst,
10 ein Stück Fleisch, ein Riesenstück Fleisch.
11 Ich kaufe einen Sack Kartoffeln,
12 einen Kasten Bier,
13 einen halben Liter Milch,
14 eine Zweiliterflasche Wein, eine Kiste Wein,
15 ein Dutzend Austern,
16 eine Schachtel Zigaretten.

Quantities

1 How much (many)?
2 I am drinking a cup of coffee,
3 a bottle of wine,
4 a glass of water,
5 a cognac, a double whisky.
6 I am eating a slice of bread,
7 a bar, a piece of chocolate,
8 half an apple,
9 a few slices of sausage meat,
10 a piece of meat, a huge piece of meat.
11 I am buying a sack of potatoes,
12 a crate of beer,
13 a pint of milk,
14 a two-litre bottle of wine, a crate of wine,
15 a dozen oysters,
16 a packet of cigarettes.

Maße, Gewichte

1 Ich brauche drei Meter Stoff.
2 Ich brauche hier dreißig Zentimeter Tesafilm.
3 Der Tisch ist 1,20 (einen Meter zwanzig) lang, achtzig breit und siebzig hoch.

Weights, Measures

1 I want three yards of material.
2 Here I need twelve inches of Cellotape.
3 The table is four feet long, two feet eight inches wide and two feet four inches high.

4 Der Schrank ist eins fünfund-dreißig breit, achtzig tief und zwei zehn hoch.	4 The cupboard is four feet six inches wide, two feet eight inches deep and seven feet tall.
5 Der Schinken wiegt über zwei Kilo: vier Pfund und hundert Gramm.	5 The ham weighs more than 2¼ lbs. (pounds): 2 lbs. 6 oz. (ounces).

Geld / Money

1 Was kostet das? Wieviel kostet das?	1 What does that cost? How much does that cost?
2 Ich kann nicht soviel ausgeben.	2 I can't spend that much.
3 Das kann ich mir nicht leisten.	3 I can't afford that.
4 Das ist eine ganze Menge Geld, ein Haufen Geld.	4 That's a lot of money, a stack of money.
5 Ich muß jetzt sparen, sonst komme ich nicht aus.	5 I must economise now, otherwise I shan't make ends meet.
6 Ich brauche nicht viel zum Leben.	6 I don't need much to live.
7 Ich habe nicht soviel dabei.	7 I haven't got as much as that on me.
8 Sie können ja anzahlen.	8 You can pay a deposit.
9 Können Sie mir etwas leihen/ borgen?	9 Can you lend me some money?
10 Ich kaufe nicht gern auf Raten.	10 I don't like buying on instal-ments, on hire purchase, on H.P.
11 Können Sie wechseln?	11 Can you change?
12 Ich kann Ihnen nicht heraus-geben.	12 I can't change that.
13 Können Sie es nicht recht machen?	13 Haven't you got right money?
14 Ich habe es leider nicht klein.	14 I'm afraid I haven't anything smaller.
15 Wie hoch steht die Mark?	15 What's the exchange rate of the mark?

16	Der Kurs ist zur Zeit ganz gut.	16	At the moment the exchange rate is quite good.

Zeit

Time

1	Wieviel Uhr ist es? Wie spät ist es?	1	What's the time?
2	Es ist eins/ein Uhr, viertel nach eins.	2	It's one/one o'clock, a quarter past one.
3	Halb zwei. Es ist halb.	3	Half past one. It's half past.
4	Dreiviertel zwei. Es ist viertel vor zwei.	4	A quarter to two. It's a quarter to.
5	Es ist fünf vor halb zwei. Es ist fünf vor halb.	5	It is 25 minutes past one. It is 25 past.
6	Es ist zehn nach halb vier. Es ist zehn nach halb.	6	It is twenty to four. It is twenty to.
7	Wie spät haben Sie? Haben Sie genaue Zeit?	7	What time do you make it? Have you the right time?
8	Die Uhr geht vor. Die Uhr geht nach.	8	The clock is fast. The clock is slow.
9	Um wieviel Uhr? Wann?	9	At what time? When?
10	Um eins. Um Punkt eins.	10	At one. On the stroke of one.
11	Vor sechs. Gegen sechs. Bis spätestens sechs.	11	Before six. About six. By six.
12	Nach sieben. Nicht vor sieben. Ab sieben.	12	After seven. Not before seven. After seven.
13	Was ist heute? Was haben wir heute (für einen Tag)?	13	What day is it today?
14	Der wievielte ist heute?	14	What is the date today?
15	Heute ist der zehnte.	15	Today's the tenth.
16	Wann?	16	When?
17	Vorgestern, gestern, heute, morgen, übermorgen.	17	The day before yesterday, yesterday, today, tomorrow, the day after tomorrow.
18	Heute abend.	18	This evening.

19	Gestern vormittag.	19	Yesterday morning.
20	Morgen nachmittag.	20	Tomorrow afternoon.
21	Am Vormittag, am Nachmittag, am Abend, in der Nacht.	21	In the morning, in the afternoon, in the evening, at night.
22	Im Frühjahr/Frühling.	22	In spring.
23	Im Sommer. Im Hochsommer.	23	In summer. In midsummer.
24	Im Herbst. Im Frühherbst. Im Spätherbst.	24	In autumn. In early autumn. In late autumn.
25	Im Winter. Mitten im Winter.	25	In winter. In the middle of winter/in mid-winter.
26	Ich traf ihn vergangenes Jahr/letztes Jahr.	26	I met him last year.
27	Ich traf ihn dieses Jahr. Ich habe ihn heuer getroffen.	27	I met him this year. I have met him this year.
28	Ich sehe ihn nächstes Jahr wieder.	28	I shall see him again next year.
29	Wir fahren morgen in acht Tagen.	29	We're leaving a week tomorrow.
30	Er kommt morgen in vierzehn Tagen nach.	30	He's joining us a fortnight tomorrow.
31	Er war kürzlich/neulich bei uns.	31	He visited us recently.
32	Er war vor drei Wochen hier.	32	He was here three weeks ago.
33	Er war gestern vor 14 Tagen bei uns.	33	He visited us a fortnight yesterday.
34	Ich habe ihn seit vierzehn Tagen nicht gesehen.	34	I haven't seen him for two weeks.
35	Ich habe ihn seit damals/seitdem nicht gesehen.	35	I haven't seen him since.
36	Ich habe ihn ewig lang nicht gesehen.	36	I haven't seen him for ages.
37	Das ist schon lange her.	37	That was a long time ago.
38	Früher war das alles ganz anders.	38	That all used to be quite different.
39	Heute hat man viel mehr Möglichkeiten.	39	Today there are a lot more opportunities.

40	Heutzutage spielt das keine so große Rolle mehr.	40	Nowadays that's not so important any more.
41	Das eilt nicht. Das hat Zeit.	41	It's not urgent. It can wait.
42	Lassen Sie sich ruhig Zeit!	42	Take your time over it.
43	Nur nichts überstürzen!	43	Don't rush it.
44	Wir sind ja noch früh dran.	44	We've still got plenty of time.
45	Wir haben noch genug Zeit, um alles zu erledigen.	45	We still have time to see to everything.
46	Es ist Zeit zu gehen.	46	It's time to go.
47	Ich möchte nicht zu spät kommen.	47	I shouldn't like to arrive late.
48	Tut mir leid, daß ich so spät komme.	48	I'm sorry to be so late.
49	Es ist leider sehr spät geworden.	49	I'm afraid it's got rather late.
50	Wann fängt es an? Wann geht es los?	50	When does it start?
51	Ist es noch nicht zu Ende? Ist es noch nicht aus?	51	Isn't it over yet? Hasn't it finished yet?
52	Wie lange brauchen Sie? Ich darf keine Zeit verlieren.	52	How long do you need? I mustn't waste any time.
53	Ich bin gleich fertig. Sie können drauf warten.	53	I'll be ready in a minute. You can wait for it.
54	Es dauert nicht lange.	54	It won't last long.
55	Ich kann inzwischen etwas anderes erledigen.	55	I can be doing something else in the meantime.
56	Man muß die Zeit ausnützen.	56	You must use the time.
57	Ich werde mir die Zeit schon vertreiben.	57	I'll find some way of passing the time.
58	Ich werde die Zeit schon irgendwie totschlagen.	58	I shall kill the time somehow or other.

Farben

1 hellblau, hellgrün, hellgrau, hellbraun

Colours

1 light blue, light green, light grey, light brown

2	dunkelrot, dunkelgrün, dunkel-blau, dunkelbraun	2	dark red, dark green, dark blue, dark brown
3	rötlich, bläulich, gelblich.	3	reddish, bluish, yellowish.
4	Er hat graublaue Augen.	4	He has grey-blue eyes.
5	Er trägt ein rotkariertes Hemd.	5	He is wearing a red check shirt.
6	Sie hat eine hübsche rot-weiß gestreifte Bluse.	6	She has a pretty blouse in red and white stripes.
7	Ich fotografiere immer schwarz-weiß.	7	I always photograph in black and white.

Verabredung

Meeting People

1	Wann können wir uns sehen/treffen?	1	When can we meet?
2	Ich kann mich morgen frei machen.	2	I can get off tomorrow.
3	Morgen abend wäre ich frei.	3	I am free tomorrow evening.
4	Ich kann es mir einrichten.	4	I can arrange it.
5	Wann paßt es Ihnen am besten?	5	When does it suit you best?
6	Wann es Ihnen paßt.	6	Whenever it suits you.
7	Ich richte mich ganz nach Ihnen.	7	I'll be guided by you.
8	Wie wäre es morgen mittag?	8	What about tomorrow at 12 o'clock?
9	Wir könnten zusammen essen.	9	We could have lunch together.
10	Also, bleibt's dabei?	10	So let's leave it like that, shall we?
11	Ich kann nächste Woche leider nicht.	11	I'm afraid I can't manage next week.
12	Vielleicht ein andermal.	12	Perhaps another time.
13	Es ergibt sich sicher eine Gelegenheit.	13	We may have an oppurtunity some time.
14	Sagen Sie bitte Herrn M., ich erwarte ihn morgen.	14	Please tell Mr. M. I'm expecting him tomorrow.

15	Sagen Sie bitte Herrn M., ich komme um 5 vorbei.	15	Please tell Mr. M. I shall call by at 5.
16	Ich soll Ihnen ausrichten, daß Herr A. Sie erwartet.	16	I've been asked to tell you that Mr. A. is expecting you.
17	Ich soll Ihnen bestellen, daß Herr A. um 5 vorbeikommt.	17	I've been asked to tell you that Mr. A. is calling by at 5.
18	Ich habe Herrn M. leider nicht angetroffen.	18	I'm afraid I didn't meet Mr. M..
19	Ich war angemeldet, aber er mußte plötzlich weg.	19	I had an appointment, but he had to leave suddenly.
20	Er war in einer Sitzung.	20	He had a meeting.
21	Er mußte zu einer dringenden Besprechung.	21	He had to go to an urgent meeting.
22	Ich habe bei seiner Sekretärin hinterlassen, wo er mich erreichen kann.	22	I've left a message with his secretary saying where he can reach me.
23	Ich habe hinterlassen, er möchte mich im Hotel anrufen.	23	I've left a message saying he can ring me at the hotel.
24	Seine Sekretärin gibt ihm Bescheid.	24	His secretary will give him the message.

Einladung

Invitation

1	Kommen Sie doch mal vorbei! Kommen Sie doch mal zu uns!	1	Do call on us. Do visit us some time.
2	Es wäre nett, wenn Sie am Sonntag kommen könnten.	2	It would be nice if you could come on Sunday.
3	Sie bringen doch Ihre Frau mit?	3	You'll bring your wife along, won't you?
4	Wir kommen gern, aber nach dem Essen.	4	We should like to come, but after the meal.
5	Ich möchte nicht, daß Ihre Frau sich soviel Arbeit macht.	5	I shouldn't like to give your wife so much trouble.
6	Mein Gott, die schönen Blumen!	6	Oh, what lovely flowers!

7 Das wäre wirklich nicht nötig gewesen. Aber, warum haben Sie sich solche Umstände gemacht?	7 That really wasn't necessary. Why did you go to so much trouble?
8 Auf Wiedersehen, vielen Dank für die Einladung!	8 Good-bye, thank you for the invitation.
9 Es war wirklich sehr nett.	9 It was really very nice.
10 Es hat uns wirklich gefreut, daß Sie gekommen sind.	10 We were really pleased you came. It was so nice having you.
11 Kommen Sie doch bald mal wieder!	11 Do come again soon.
12 Jetzt müssen Sie aber auch mal zu uns kommen.	12 But this time you must come to us.
13 Meine Mutter würde Sie auch gern kennenlernen.	13 My mother would like to meet you, too.
14 Ich bringe Sie noch runter.	14 I'll see you downstairs.
15 Kommen Sie gut nach Haus!	15 I hope you get home safely.

Vorstellung

Introduction

1 Darf ich vorstellen: Herr Huber – Frau Dr. Engl.	1 May I introduce Mr. Huber, Dr. Engl.
2 Freut mich, Sie kennenzulernen.	2 How do you do?
3 Ich habe schon viel von Ihnen gehört.	3 I've heard a lot about you.
4 Ach, Sie sind der Herr aus Stuttgart!	4 Oh yes, you're the gentleman from Stuttgart.
5 Frau Dr. Engl, darf ich Ihnen Herrn Huber vorstellen?	5 Dr. Engl, may I introduce Mr. Huber to you?
6 Kennen Sie schon Herrn Huber? – Das ist Frau Dr. Engl.	6 Do you know Mr. Huber? – This is Dr. Engl.
7 Darf ich bekannt machen?	7 May I introduce you.

Personenbeschreibung	Descriptions of People
1 Wie ist er/sie? Wie sieht er aus?	1 What is he/she like? What does he/she look like?
2 Er ist nett. Er sieht nett aus.	2 He's nice. He looks nice.
3 Er sieht gut aus.	3 He is good looking.
4 Sie ist hübsch. – Sie ist häßlich.	4 She is pretty. – She's ugly.
5 Sie ist apart.	5 She has something about her.
6 Sie ist sehr gepflegt/ungepflegt.	6 She is very well groomed/unkempt.
7 Sie ist schlank/etwas vollschlank.	7 She is slim/a bit plump.
8 Sie ist ein wenig rundlich. Sie ist dick.	8 She's a little plump. She is fat.
9 Er ist ziemlich groß/klein.	9 He's fairly tall/short.
10 Er ist kräftig.	10 He is strong.
11 Er ist ein sportlicher Typ.	11 He's a sporting type.
12 Er ist 50, aber er sieht jünger/älter aus.	12 He's 50, but he looks younger/older.
13 Er ist ein Typ, der auf Frauen wirkt.	13 He is the sort who impresses women.
14 Er ist 18, aber er wirkt noch nicht sehr erwachsen.	14 He's 18, but he still doesn't make a very adult impression.
15 Sie ist schon eine junge Dame.	15 She's already a young lady.
16 Er weiß sich zu benehmen. Er benimmt sich tadellos.	16 He knows how to behave. He has perfect manners.
17 Er ist gesellschaftlich sehr gewandt.	17 He knows how to behave in company.
18 Er hat keine Kinderstube. Er hat keine Manieren.	18 He was badly brought up. He has no manners.
19 Er benimmt sich leider oft daneben.	19 Unfortunately he often behaves badly.
20 Sie ist immer gut angezogen.	20 She is always well dressed.
21 Sie ist sehr elegant.	21 She is very elegant.
22 Sie ist sehr schick.	22 She is very smart.

23	Sie hat Geschmack. Sie hat einen guten Geschmack.	23	She has taste. She has good taste.
24	Sie ist ein bißchen altmodisch.	24	She is a little old-fashioned.
25	Sie ist eine typische Deutsche/Engländerin/Amerikanerin.	25	She is a typical German/Englishwoman/American.
26	Wie ist er/sie menschlich?	26	What is he/she like as a person?
27	Wie ist er/sie im Wesen?	27	What is his/her character like?
28	Er ist nett, sympathisch, ein feiner Kerl.	28	He is nice, likeable, a good chap.
29	Er ist sehr hilfsbereit und kameradschaftlich.	29	He is very helpful and friendly.
30	Er ist rücksichtsvoll. – Er ist manchmal rücksichtslos.	30	He is considerate. – He is sometimes inconsiderate.
31	Er ist taktvoll. – Er ist manchmal taktlos.	31	He is tactful. – He is sometimes tactless.
32	Er ist großzügig. – Er ist geizig.	32	He is generous. – He is mean.
33	Er ist stur.	33	He is stubborn.
34	Er ist sehr vernünftig. Man kann mit ihm reden.	34	He is very sensible. You can talk to him.
35	Er ist ruhig. – Er ist nervös.	35	He is quiet. – He is nervous.
36	Er ist bescheiden und zurückhaltend.	36	He is modest and reserved.
37	Er ist überspannt, eingebildet, arrogant.	37	He is eccentric, conceited, arrogant.
38	Er ist ein Angeber. Er gibt gern an.	38	He shows off. He likes to show off.
39	Er ist interessant.	39	He is interesting.
40	Er ist langweilig, fade, nichtssagend.	40	He is boring, dull, colourless.
41	Er ist fröhlich, heiter, lustig. – Er ist ernst.	41	He is jolly, gay, cheerful. – He is serious.
42	Er ist sehr sicher und frei im Auftreten.	42	He is very self-assured and free and easy.
43	Er ist schüchtern und unsicher. Er ist gehemmt.	43	He is shy and unsure of himself. He is inhibited.

44	Er ist sehr empfindlich und immer gleich beleidigt.	44	He is very sensitive and easily takes offence.
45	Er hat eine dicke Haut.	45	He is thick-skinned.
46	Er ist humorlos. Er versteht keinen Spaß. Er nimmt alles gleich übel.	46	He has no sense of humour. He can't take a joke. He always feels insulted.
47	Kann er/sie etwas? Wie ist er/sie im Beruf?	47	Is he/she a capable person? Is he/she good at his/her job?
48	Er ist sehr ehrgeizig.	48	He's very ambitious.
49	Er kann etwas auf seinem Gebiet.	49	He is very capable in his subject.
50	Er wird es sicher zu etwas bringen.	50	He'll certainly go far.
51	Er kann mit den Leuten umgehen.	51	He knows how to deal with people.
52	Er kann sich durchsetzen.	52	He can get his way.
53	Er wirkt überzeugend.	53	He seems convincing.
54	Ich finde, er macht zu wenig aus sich.	54	I think he isn't ambitious enough.
55	Er ist vielseitig begabt.	55	He's a man of many talents.
56	Er ist besonders für Sprachen begabt.	56	He's especially talented for languages.
57	Er spricht fließend Deutsch. Er spricht ganz akzentfrei.	57	He speaks fluent German. He speaks without any accent.
58	Er ist musikalisch. Er ist eminent musikalisch.	58	He is musical. He is outstandingly musical.
59	Er ist sehr gebildet.	59	He is very well educated.
60	Er hat viel gesehen und gelesen. Er hat viel erlebt.	60	He has seen and read a lot. He's had a lot of experience.
61	Er ist schon viel herumgekommen.	61	He's been around a lot.

Persönliches Verhältnis

Personal Relations

1	Ich finde ihn sehr nett. Ich finde sie reizend.	1	I think he's very nice. I think she's charming.

2 Ich kenne ihn/sie gut. Wir kennen uns schon lange.	2 I know him/her well. We've known each other for a long time.
3 Wir sind gute Freunde. Wir sind sehr gut befreundet.	3 We're good friends. We're on very friendly terms.
4 Die beiden passen gut zusammen.	4 They're both well suited to each other.
5 Sie verstehen sich sehr gut.	5 They get on well together.
6 Ich komme sehr gut mit meinen Kollegen aus.	6 I get on very well with my colleagues.
7 Ich mag ihn nicht. Ich finde ihn schrecklich.	7 I don't like him. I think he's terrible.
8 Er liegt mir nicht.	8 He's not my type.
9 Wir können uns nicht leiden/ausstehen/riechen.	9 We can't stand/bear/bear the sight of/each other.
10 Er haßt mich wie die Pest.	10 He hates me like poison.

Wetter, Klima

Weather, Climate

1 Wie ist das Wetter heute?	1 What is the weather like today?
2 Schöner Tag heute. Herrlich! Wunderbar!	2 Lovely day today. Marvellous. Wonderful.
3 Es könnte nicht schöner sein!	3 It couldn't be better.
4 Strahlende Sonne und doch nicht zu heiß.	4 Brilliant sunshine and yet not too hot.
5 Es ist recht schön/ganz schön heute, finden Sie nicht?	5 It's quite nice/rather nice today, don't you think?
6 Gerade recht zum Laufen, aber noch nichts zum Baden.	6 Just right for walking, but not hot enough for bathing yet.
7 Und bei diesem Wetter muß man arbeiten! Eine Schande!	7 And we have to work in this weather! A disgrace!
8 Wie war's denn bei Ihnen?	8 What was it like where you were, then?
9 Schlecht! Regnerisch, schwül, gewittrig, unbeständig.	9 Bad. Rainy, sultry, thundery, changeable.

10	Abends war es sogar manchmal neblig.	10	In the evenings it was even foggy sometimes.
11	Und dann war es wieder ziemlich kühl.	11	And then it was rather cool again.
12	Zu kühl zum Draußensitzen.	12	Too cool to sit outside.
13	Tolles Gewitter! Das blitzt und donnert!	13	Marvellous thunderstorm, with the thunder and lightning.
14	Schauen Sie, wie es regnet!	14	Look how it's raining.
15	Was heißt da: regnet? Es gießt!	15	What do you mean raining? It's pouring.
16	Gestern hat es im Gebirge schon geschneit.	16	Yesterday it even snowed in the mountains.
17	Heute nacht soll es frieren, bis fünf unter Null.	17	Tonight it's supposed to be going to freeze, down to minus five (degrees centigrade).
18	Morgen taut es sicher wieder.	18	It'll certainly thaw again tomorrow.
19	Richtiges Grippewetter, viel zu warm für Januar.	19	Real 'flu' weather, much too warm for January.
20	Es schneit, aber der Schnee bleibt nicht liegen.	20	It's snowing, but the snow isn't settling.
21	Wie ist der Wetterbericht?	21	What does the weather forecast say?
22	Nicht besonders. Es wird wieder schlecht.	22	Nothing special. It's going to be bad again.
23	Der Wetterbericht ist gut, es wird wärmer.	23	The weather forecast is good, it's going to get warmer.
24	Haben Sie den Straßenzustandsbericht gehört?	24	Have you heard the road report?
25	Auf den meisten Pässen ist Glatteis.	25	There is ice on most of the mountain passes.
26	Zum Teil liegt Neuschnee.	26	In places there's fresh snow.
27	Wir brauchen Schneeketten.	27	We need snow chains.
28	Das Wetter/Klima hier ist schrecklich.	28	The weather/climate here is terrible.
29	Es bekommt mir gar nicht gut.	29	It doesn't agree with me at all.

30	Nachts friere ich, am Tag schwitze ich.	30 I freeze at night and sweat during the day.
31	Das Wetter macht mich ganz kaputt.	31 The weather's killing me.
32	Spüren Sie das Wetter nicht?	32 Doesn't the weather affect you?
33	Ich finde es herrlich hier.	33 I think it's wonderful here.
34	Für mich ist das Klima hier genau das Richtige.	34 The climate here is just right for me.
35	Mir tut es richtig gut.	35 It really does me good.
36	Nicht einmal der Föhn macht mir zu schaffen.	36 Not even the foehn gives me any trouble. (Foehn – warm southerly wind in the Alps)

Gesundes und ungesundes Leben

Good Health and Ill Health

1	Ich lebe gesund.	1 I live a healthy life.
2	Ich tue etwas für meine Gesundheit.	2 I do something about my health.
3	Ich lebe sehr regelmäßig.	3 I lead a very regular life.
4	Ich bin vorsichtig mit Kaffee und Alkohol.	4 I'm careful with coffee and alcohol.
5	Das Rauchen habe ich mir ganz abgewöhnt.	5 I've given up smoking altogether.
6	Ich nehme mir Zeit zum Essen, das ist wichtig!	6 I take time over my meals, that's important.
7	Ich achte sehr auf die schlanke Linie.	7 I watch my figure very carefully.
8	Und jeden Tag kalt duschen, das hält jung!	8 And a cold shower every day, that keeps you young.
9	Wir essen viel Obst und Gemüse, wegen der Vitamine.	9 We eat a lot of fruit and vegetables, because of the vitamins.
10	Man braucht ja deshalb kein reiner Vegetarier zu sein!	10 But that doesn't mean you have to be an all-out vegetarian.

11	Treiben Sie auch viel Sport?	11	Do you do a lot of sport, too?
12	Ich mache viel Gymnastik.	12	I do a lot of gymnastics.
13	Ich lebe sehr ungesund, aber was soll ich machen?	13	I live a very unhealthy life, but what can I do?
14	Ich bin immer im Druck.	14	I'm always under pressure of work.
15	Dann die Unregelmäßigkeit: mal früh essen, mal spät!	15	And then everything's so irregular: sometimes I eat early, sometimes late.
16	Das Essen stürze ich in fünf Minuten hinunter.	16	I gulp my food down in five minutes.
17	Das muß sich ja irgendwann rächen.	17	That's bound to have its effects some time.
18	Und dann immer im Auto! Keine Bewegung!	18	And then I'm always in the car! No exercise.
19	Sie sehen ja, wie ich dick werde!	19	You can see how fat I'm getting.
20	Das geht natürlich aufs Herz.	20	Of course, that affects your heart.
21	Zum Sport komme ich auch nicht mehr.	21	I never get round to doing any sport nowadays.
22	Bei den Besprechungen raucht man und trinkt man.	22	At the conferences everyone smokes and drinks.
23	Oft auf nüchternen Magen!	23	Often on an empty stomach.
24	Und keine Nacht vor zwei ins Bett!	24	I never get to bed before two.
25	Wem sagen Sie das! Ich müßte auch mal ausspannen.	25	It's just the same with me. I really should relax sometimes, too.

Glück und Pech im Leben   Good and Bad Luck in Life

1	Sie sind ein Glückspilz. Sie haben immer Glück.	1	You're a lucky fellow. You're always lucky.
2	Ich beneide Sie.	2	I envy you.

3	Sie haben es geschafft. Ich gratuliere!		3	You've done it. Congratulations!
4	Sie haben es zu etwas gebracht.		4	You've got somewhere.
5	**Sie sind ein Pechvogel!** Sie haben so viel Pech!		5	You're an unlucky fellow. You have so much bad luck.
6	Sie sind wirklich nicht zu beneiden.		6	I really don't envy you.
7	Sie haben wirklich viel durchzumachen.		7	You really have a lot to put up with.
8	Sie haben es schwer, ich weiß.		8	You have a hard time of it, I know.
9	**Aber Sie dürfen nicht aufgeben!**		9	But you mustn't give up.
10	Sie dürfen jetzt den Mut nicht verlieren.		10	You mustn't lose heart now.
11	Das wird schon wieder!		11	Things will look up again.
12	Es kommt auch wieder anders!		12	Things will take a turn for the better.

Haus und Wohnung

House and Home

1	Wo wohnen Sie? Wie wohnen Sie?		1	Where do you live? How do you live?
2	Wir haben ein kleines Haus mit Garten, etwas außerhalb.		2	We have a small house with a garden, a bit outside the town.
3	Das hat viel für sich. Das hat viele Vorteile.		3	There's a lot to be said for that. There are many advantages in that.
4	Man muß nicht immer Rücksicht auf die anderen nehmen.		4	You don't always have to consider the others.
5	Andererseits ist es ziemlich abgelegen.		5	On the other hand, it's rather off the beaten track.
6	Man kann eben nicht alles haben.		6	But you can't have everything.

7	Unsere Wohnung liegt sehr verkehrsgünstig.	7	Our flat is very conveniently situated for transport.
8	Sie liegt wirklich ideal.	8	It's really in the ideal location.
9	Die Verbindung ist ausgezeichnet.	9	The connection is excellent.
10	In zehn Minuten bin ich im Zentrum.	10	I'm in the centre (of town) in ten minutes.
11	Das würde man nicht denken, so ruhig ist es hier!	11	You wouldn't think so; it's so quiet here.
12	Ist das eine Eigentumswohnung? Nein, gemietet.	12	Is the flat your own property? No, rented.
13	Ich habe nur ein Zimmer.	13	I only have a room.
14	Wozu eine Wohnung für mich allein?	14	What's the use of a flat for me alone?
15	Die Leute sind recht nett.	15	The people are very nice.
16	Die Hausfrau ist ein bißchen komisch, aber ...	16	The landlady is a bit funny, but ...
17	Sie kümmert sich nicht weiter um mich.	17	She doesn't bother about me at all.
18	Ich bin ganz unabhängig.	18	I'm completely independent.
19	Kennen Sie die Wohnung von Meiers? Einfach toll!	19	Do you know Meiers' flat? Simply marvellous!
20	Schon das Haus ist hochherrschaftlich, ganz feudal!	20	The building itself is magnificent, quite sumptuous.
21	Helle, sonnige Zimmer, alles mit Blick auf den Park.	21	Bright, sunny rooms, all with a view of the park.
22	Und die Einrichtung! Modern und doch gemütlich.	22	And the furnishings! Modern and yet comfortable.
23	Es sind viereinhalb Zimmer.	23	There are four main rooms, and a smaller one.
24	Und die Küche – mit allen Schikanen!	24	And the kitchen – every conceivable gadget!
25	Man merkt schon sehr, daß Hubers Neureiche sind.	25	You really can see that Hubers are nouveaux riches.
26	So etwas Protziges!	26	So showy!

27 Die ganze Einrichtung ist teuer und geschmacklos.	27 All the furniture is expensive and in bad taste.
28 Und die Bilder – so etwas von Kitsch!	28 And the pictures – such trash!
29 Aber das Schlafzimmer sollten Sie erst mal sehen!	29 But you should see the bedroom!
30 Aha, das ist also Ihr Zuhause. Hübsch!	30 I see, so this is where you live. Nice place.
31 Ja, die Bude ist ganz hübsch geworden.	31 Yes, the room's turned out quite pretty.
32 Man kann mit einfachen Mitteln allerhand machen.	32 You can do all sorts of things without much outlay.
33 Das Zimmer war so lieblos möbliert.	33 The room was furnished in such an impersonal way.
34 Ein kleines Kissen, eine hübsche Sofadecke, ein süßer kleiner Spiegel, und schon hat es irgendwie Stil.	34 A little cushion, a pretty sofa cover, a nice little mirror, and the place has a certain style about it.
35 Die Miete ist erschwinglich.	35 The rent is reasonable.
36 Für heutzutage ist das wirklich spottbillig!	36 That's really dirt cheap as things go today.
37 Um die Heizung muß ich mich nicht kümmern.	37 I don't have to bother about the heating.
38 Ich habe einen kleinen Ölofen, das ist kein Problem.	38 I have a little oil stove, there's no problem there.
39 Einmal in der Woche wird saubergemacht.	39 The place is cleaned once a week.
40 Sonst mache ich das Zimmer selbst.	40 Apart from that, I do the room myself.
41 Wir wollen ein Haus bauen.	41 We want to build a house.
42 Wir haben schon lang einen Bausparvertrag.	42 We have had a building society savings account for a long time now.
43 Das Grundstück habe ich von meinen Eltern.	43 I got the land from my parents.

44	Wohnzimmer unten, Schlafzimmer und Bad oben?	44	Living-room downstairs, bedrooms and bathroom upstairs?
45	Nein, einen Bungalow. Alles ebenerdig ist praktischer.	45	No, a bungalow. It's more practical having everything on ground level.
46	Warum nehmen Sie kein Fertighaus?	46	Why don't you have a factory-made house?
47	Ich habe ganz bestimmte Vorstellungen von der Einteilung.	47	I have quite definite ideas about the arrangement of the rooms.

Hausfrau, Haushalt   *Housewife, Household*

1	Haben Sie Ihren Beruf ganz aufgegeben?	1	Have you given up your job altogether?
2	Ich kann neben dem Haushalt nichts mehr machen.	2	I can't do anything apart from the housework.
3	So ein Haushalt will geführt sein!	3	A house like this needs some looking after.
4	Die Kinder wollen versorgt sein, der Mann auch.	4	The children have to be looked after, my husband as well.
5	Dann heißt es aufräumen, staubsaugen	5	Then there's the tidying up, vacuuming (vacuum cleaning)
6	einkaufen	6	shopping
7	waschen, bügeln	7	washing, ironing
8	kochen, Geschirr spülen	8	cooking, washing up
9	Kinderkleider nähen	9	sewing the children's clothes
10	zerrissene Hosen flicken	10	mending torn trousers
11	Knöpfe annähen.	11	sewing on buttons.
12	Am Abend soll alles tipptopp sein.	12	By the evening everything has to be ship-shape.
13	Und eine Hilfe bekommt man auch schwer.	13	And it's very difficult to find any help.
14	Aber man kann sich heute manches leichter machen.	14	But nowadays you can take the hard work out of some of the jobs.

15 Ich habe wirklich alle Geräte, die man haben kann:	15 I have really all the appliances it's possible to have:
16 Die vollautomatische Waschmaschine.	16 a fully automatic washing-machine.
17 Die große Wäsche gebe ich aus.	17 I send out the main washing.
18 eine Bügelmaschine	18 an ironing machine
19 Für kleinere Sachen nehme ich das Bügeleisen.	19 For smaller things I use the iron.
20 einen ganz neuen Staubsauger	20 a brand-new vacuum cleaner
21 einen Mixer und einen Entsafter	21 a mixer and a juice extractor
22 Ich kaufe allerdings Saft lieber in Dosen.	22 But I prefer to buy juice in cans.
23 einen Toaster/Toaströster	23 a toaster
24 einen ganz modernen Elektroherd.	24 a very modern electric stove.
25 Am Wochenende gehen wir natürlich oft essen.	25 At weekends, of course, we often eat out.
26 eine Zickzackmaschine	26 a zig-zag sewing-machine
27 Schneidern will ich nicht, aber für Kindersachen ...	27 I don't like making clothes, but for the children's things ...

Essen / Meals

1 Ich frühstücke wie die meisten Deutschen.	1 I have the same for breakfast as most Germans.
2 Kaffee, Honig- oder Marmeladebrote.	2 Coffee, bread and honey or jam.
3 Manchmal gibt es auch frische Brötchen/Semmeln.	3 Sometimes, I also have fresh rolls.
4 Am Sonntag gibt es ein weiches Ei oder ein Spiegelei.	4 On Sundays, I have a soft boiled egg or a fried egg.
5 Das englische Frühstück ist anders.	5 The English breakfast is different.
6 Zuerst essen wir Haferflocken oder Corn Flakes mit Milch und Zucker.	6 First we have porridge or corn flakes with milk and sugar.

7	Dann essen wir Schinken mit Ei oder Rührei auf Toast.	7	Then we have ham and eggs or scrambled eggs on toast.
8	Am Schluß essen wir Toast mit Orangenmarmelade.	8	To finish with we have toast and marmalade.
9	Zum Mittagessen haben wir oft Fleisch.	9	For lunch we often have meat.
10	Was gibt es denn heute?	10	What is there today then?
11	Einen Braten mit Kartoffeln und Erbsen.	11	A roast with potatoes and peas.
12	Nudeln mit Tomatensoße und grünem Salat.	12	Spaghetti with tomato sauce and lettuce.
13	Kartoffelbrei mit Rührei und Schinken.	13	Mashed potatoes with scrambled eggs and bacon.
14	Kotelett oder Schnitzel mit Beilagen.	14	Chop or cutlet with vegetables.
15	Fisch mit Salzkartoffeln und zerlassener Butter.	15	Fish with boiled potatoes and melted butter.
16	Heute gibt es aus der Dose/ Büchse: Ravioli oder so ...	16	Today there is tinned ravioli or something ...
17	Die tiefgekühlten Sachen schmecken übrigens wie frisch.	17	The deep-frozen foods, by the way, taste like fresh ones.
18	Zum Nachtisch Pudding oder Obst.	18	For dessert blancmange or fruit.
19	Oder Erdbeeren mit Schlagsahne.	19	Or strawberries and whipped cream.
20	Abends gibt es oft kalt, besonders im Sommer.	20	In the evenings we often have a cold meal, especially in the summer.
21	Ein bißchen Aufschnitt, ein bißchen Käse.	21	An assortment of sliced sausage meat, a little cheese.

Trinken

Drinking

1	Was wollen Sie trinken?	1	What do you want to drink?
2	Kaffee, Tee, Schokolade, Milch.	2	Coffee, tea, chocolate, milk.

#	German	#	English
3	Helles oder dunkles Bier, Weißwein, Rotwein.	3	Lager or brown ale, white wine, red wine.
4	Mineralwasser, Limonade.	4	Mineral water, lemonade.
5	Apfelsaft, Traubensaft, Johannisbeersaft.	5	Apple juice, grape juice, black currant juice.
6	Orangensaft natur.	6	Natural orange juice.
7	Oder etwas Alkohol?	7	Or something alcoholic?
8	Kognak, Whisky, Gin?	8	Cognac, whisky, gin?
9	Oder etwas Gemixtes?	9	Or a mixed drink?
10	Ich trinke den Kaffee schwarz.	10	I drink my coffee black.
11	Den Whisky bitte pur, mit Eis, für meine Frau mit Soda.	11	The whisky neat please, with ice, with soda for my wife.
12	Das Bier bitte nicht ganz kalt.	12	The beer not too cold, please.
13	Der Wein hat gerade die rechte Temperatur.	13	The wine is just the right temperature.
14	Den Wein müßte man kälter servieren.	14	The wine should be served colder.
15	Zum Fisch weißen, zum Braten roten Wein, bitte.	15	White wine with the fish, red wine with the roast, please.
16	Darf ich auf Ihr Wohl anstoßen?	16	May I drink to your health?
17	Prost! / Wohl bekomm's! / Zum Wohlsein!	17	Cheers!
18	Alkohol bekommt mir nicht.	18	Alcohol doesn't agree with me.
19	Der Wein ist mir gestern nicht gut bekommen.	19	The wine didn't agree with me yesterday.
20	Ich vertrage nichts mehr.	20	I can't take any more.
21	Der Wein ist ihm in den Kopf gestiegen.	21	The wine went to his head.
22	Ich finde, bei Whisky behält man einen klaren Kopf.	22	I find that with whisky you keep a clear head.
23	Ich habe einen Kater.	23	I have a hangover.
24	Man merkt Ihnen aber nichts an.	24	You don't show it.

25 Er ist betrunken. Er weiß nicht mehr, was er sagt.	25 He is drunk. He doesn't know what he's saying any more.
26 Ein kleiner Schwips kann herrlich sein!	26 It can be a marvellous feeling to be a bit tipsy.
27 Ich glaube, ich bin beschwipst.	27 I think I've had one over the eight.

Rauchen

Smoking

1 Rauchen Sie? Was rauchen Sie?	1 Do you smoke? What do you smoke?
2 Danke, ich bin Nichtraucher. Ich rauche nicht.	2 No, thank you. I'm a non-smoker. I don't smoke.
3 Ich rauche Zigaretten. Ich rauche Zigarre/Zigarren.	3 I smoke cigarettes. I smoke cigars.
4 Ich rauche nur mit Filter.	4 I only smoke filter cigarettes.
5 Ich rauche nur Schwarze / schwarze Zigaretten.	5 I only smoke cigarettes made of dark tobacco.
6 Bei der Arbeit rauche ich Pfeife.	6 At work I smoke a pipe.
7 Ich habe einen herrlichen englischen Tabak.	7 I have some wonderful English tobacco.
8 Riechen Sie mal. Wollen Sie ihn probieren?	8 Smell it. Would you like to try it?
9 Der Arzt sagt, ich soll das Rauchen aufgeben.	9 The doctor says I should give up smoking.
10 Ich habe schon versucht, es mir abzugewöhnen.	10 I've already tried to give it up.
11 Aber es ist schwer, darauf zu verzichten.	11 But it's difficult to do without it.
12 Eine Zigarette nach dem Essen – das gehört einfach dazu!	12 A cigarette after each meal – that's simply a must.

Bei Tisch

At Table

1 Darf ich Ihnen noch etwas Fleisch geben?	1 May I give you some more meat?

2	Gern, vielen Dank.	2	Certainly, thank you.
3	Aber wirklich nur noch ein kleines Stückchen.	3	But really only a small piece.
4	Dürfte ich Sie um ein Stück Brot bitten?	4	May I ask you for a slice of bread?
5	Würden Sie mir bitte das Salz herübergeben?	5	Would you pass me the salt, please?
6	Darf ich um die Soße bitten?	6	Could you pass me the sauce, please?
7	Bitte, Sie nehmen sich doch selbst?	7	Please help yourself, won't you?
8	Ich muß Ihnen doch nicht immer anbieten?	8	I don't have to keep offering you things, do I?
9	Sagen Sie nur, was Sie brauchen.	9	Just say what you need.
10	Wenn Ihnen etwas nicht zusagt, lassen Sie es ruhig stehen.	10	If there's anything that doesn't appeal to you, just leave it.
11	Sie sind unser Essen sicher nicht gewöhnt.	11	I expect you're not used to our food.
12	Es tut mir leid, aber ich bin kein großer Esser.	12	I'm afraid I'm not a big eater.
13	Entschuldigen Sie, ich muß mit Fett etwas aufpassen.	13	I'm sorry, but I have to be rather careful with fat.
14	Ich muß leider mit dem Magen etwas vorsichtig sein.	14	I'm afraid I have to be rather careful what I eat.
15	Meine Leber ist leider nicht ganz in Ordnung.	15	I'm afraid there's something wrong with my liver.
16	Sie haben so hübsch gedeckt!	16	You've set the table so prettily.
17	Wie hübsch Sie das alles hergerichtet haben!	17	How nicely you've got everything ready.
18	Ich sage immer: Das Auge ißt mit.	18	I always say it must look appetising.
19	Sie haben so schönes Geschirr.	19	You've got such nice crockery.
20	Das moderne Besteck paßt auch gut dazu.	20	The modern cutlery also goes very well with it.

Im Lokal

1 Die Herrschaften wünschen?
2 Die Karte bitte. Und die Getränkekarte.
3 Wir möchten gern bestellen.
4 Was können Sie uns heute empfehlen?
5 Ist das mild? Ist das sehr scharf?
6 Es ist stark gewürzt, ziemlich pikant.
7 Ich möchte nur eine Kleinigkeit.
8 Ich hätte gern etwas Leichtes.
9 Was geht denn schnell?
10 Könnte ich statt Kartoffeln Reis dazu haben?
11 Das Steak bitte englisch.
12 Für mich bitte rosa, nicht ganz durch.
13 Ein Helles/Dunkles bitte. (= ½ Liter)
14 Ein kleines Helles bitte. (= ¼ Liter)
15 Einen Schoppen Rotwein. (= ¼ Liter)
16 Herr Ober, bitte! Fräulein, bitte!
17 Die Suppe kann ich nicht essen. Sie ist ganz kalt.
18 Sie ist total versalzen.
19 Der Fisch ist nicht durch. Er ist noch halb roh.
20 Ich wollte ein 4-Minuten-Ei, das hier ist hart!

In the Restaurant

1 What would you like?
2 The menu, please. And the wine list.
3 We should like to order.
4 What can you recommend us today?
5 Is that mild? Is that very hot?
6 It is strongly spiced, fairly/ highly seasoned.
7 I only want a little.
8 I should like something light.
9 What doesn't take long then?
10 Could I have rice instead of potatoes with it?
11 The steak rare, please.
12 For me pink, please, not done right through.
13 A pint of lager/brown ale, please.
14 Half a pint of lager, please.
15 A glass of red wine.
16 Waiter! Waitress!
17 I can't eat the soup. It's quite cold.
18 It's far too salty.
19 The fish is not done. It's still half raw.
20 I wanted a four-minute egg, this one is hard.

21	Herr Ober, bitte zahlen!	21	Waiter, the bill, please.
22	Ich bin hier schon einmal rein-gefallen.	22	I've been caught out here once before.
23	Da war ich heute zum letzten-mal!	23	This is the last time I'm coming here.
24	Viel zu teuer für das, was sie bieten!	24	Much too expensive for what they offer.
25	Ein richtiges Nepplokal!	25	You have to pay through the nose at this restaurant.
26	Und diese hochnäsige Bedie-nung!	26	And this snooty service.
27	Es ist nett hier.	27	It's nice here.
28	Man ißt gut hier.	28	The food is good here.
29	Die Bedienung ist wirklich aufmerksam.	29	The waiters are really attentive.
30	Wir haben das Lokal erst kürzlich entdeckt.	30	We only discovered the restaurant recently.
31	Man kann es wirklich emp-fehlen.	31	You can really recommend it.

In verschiedenen Geschäften

In Various Shops

1	Bitte haben Sie ...? Ich hätte gern ...	1	Have you got ..., please? I would like ...
2	Ich suche ... Ich brauche ...	2	I am looking for ... I need ...
3	Ist das Brot frisch?	3	Is that loaf fresh?
4	Ich hätte lieber eines von gestern.	4	I would prefer a yesterday's.
5	Und ein Paket Zwieback, bitte.	5	And a packet of rusks, please.
6	Eine Flasche Milch.	6	A bottle of milk.
7	Zwölf Eier, bitte.	7	A dozen eggs, please.
8	Einen Viertelliter Sahne. (südd.: Schlagrahm).	8	Half a pint of cream.
9	Drei Schweineschnitzel. Bitte klopfen!	9	Three pork cutlets. Could you please beat them?

10	Hundert Gramm Aufschnitt und fünfzig von dem Schinken.	10	A quarter (of a pound) of mixed sliced sausage meat and two ounces of ham.
11	Sind die Äpfel süß? (sauer, säuerlich, saftig, mehlig).	11	Are the apples sweet? (sour, on the sour side, juicy, mealy).
12	Sind die Orangen saftig/strohig?	12	Are the oranges juicy/dry?
13	Ist der Kopfsalat frisch?	13	Is the lettuce fresh?
14	Reife Tomaten, aber nicht zu weich!	14	Ripe tomatoes, but not too soft.
15	Ich suche Schnürsenkel,	15	Shoe laces, please.
16	einen Bindfaden/eine Schnur, ein Gummiband,	16	String, an elastic band.
17	Tesafilm, Klebstreifen.	17	Cellotape, sticky tape.
18	Packpapier, einen Pappkarton.	18	Wrapping paper, a cardboard box.

Im Konfektionshaus

At the Clothes Shop

1	Ich möchte einen Anzug/ein Kostüm.	1	I should like a suit/a costume.
2	Etwas Wärmeres für den Winter und die Übergangszeit.	2	Something warmer for the winter and autumn and spring.
3	Etwas Leichtes für den Sommer.	3	Something light for the summer.
4	Er muß etwas aushalten, ich bin viel auf Reisen.	4	It must be hard-wearing, I travel around a lot.
5	Wie trägt sich der Stoff?	5	How does this material wear?
6	Knittert er leicht?	6	Does it crease easily?
7	Hält er die Form? Hält die Bügelfalte?	7	Will it keep its shape? Will the trouser creases stay in?
8	Ich finde, so etwas kann ich nicht tragen.	8	I don't think I can wear anything like that.
9	Haben Sie nicht etwas Konservativeres?	9	Haven't you something a little more conservative?

10 Ich hätte ihn gern etwas gedeckter, nicht so empfindlich.	10 I should like it a little darker, so as not to show marks so easily.
11 Das Muster ist mir zu kräftig.	11 The pattern is too distinct for me.
12 Das ist genau das, was ich suche.	12 That's exactly what I'm looking for.
13 Der sitzt wirklich wie nach Maß.	13 It really fits as if it were made to measure.
14 Ich glaube, wir müssen die Ärmel kürzen.	14 I think we'll have to shorten the sleeves.
15 Die Hose ist im Bund zu weit, wir machen sie enger.	15 The trousers are too big at the waist; let's take them in a bit.

Wäscherei und Reinigung / Laundry and Cleaner's

1 Sechs Hemden, waschen und bügeln, bitte.	1 Six shirts, wash and iron, please.
2 Wie lang dauert das?	2 How long will they take?
3 Und Expreß geht es bis morgen?	3 And will they be ready tomorrow by express service?
4 Macht das im Preis viel aus?	4 Does that make much difference to the price?
5 Und das bitte reinigen: ein Anzug, ein Regenmantel, ein Kleid, ein Anorak.	5 And that needs cleaning, please: a suit, a mackintosh, a dress, an anorak.
6 Wann kann ich die Sachen abholen?	6 When can I collect the things?

Beim Schuster / At the Shoe-Repairer's

1 Ein Paar Ledersohlen, bitte.	1 A pair of leather soles, please.
2 Schauen Sie, hat es einen Sinn, die nochmal zu richten?	2 Look, you think there's any point in repairing them again?

3 Machen Sie bitte dünne Gummiabsätze drauf.
4 Dann brauche ich noch Schnürsenkel und farblose Schuhcreme.

3 Please put thin rubber heels on these.
4 Then I also need shoe laces and colourless shoe-cream.

Auf der Post

1 Bitte zehn Dreißiger (Briefmarken zu 30 Pfennig).
2 Den Brief bitte einschreiben.
3 Und den hier per Eilboten.

4 Geht das als Päckchen oder ist es zu schwer?
5 Sind die Zahlkarten richtig ausgefüllt?

6 Und hier habe ich eine Postanweisung für Spanien.

7 Ist etwas für mich postlagernd da? Hier mein Ausweis.

At the Post Office

1 Ten threepenny stamps, please.
2 Register this letter, please.
3 And this one by express delivery.
4 Will this go as a packet or is it too heavy?
5 Are the "Zahlkarten" filled in properly? (A "*Zahlkarte*" is for payment into a Post Office account.)
6 And here is a "Postanweisung" for Spain. (A "*Postanweisung*" is something like a money order.)
7 Is there anything for me poste restante? Here is my identity card (passport).

Fernamt und Telegrafenamt

1 Ist dort die Telegrammaufnahme?
2 Bitte ein Telegramm nach London.

Telephone Exchange and Telegraph Office

1 Is that the connection for telegrams?
2 I want to send a telegram to Munich.

3 Hier ist München 22 48 79 (zwo, zwo, vier, acht, sieben, neun), Wolfgang Halm.

4 Die Adresse: Geoffrey Burwell – ich buchstabiere: Berta, Ulrich, Richard, Wilhelm, Emil, zweimal Ludwig.

5 Das deutsche Buchstabieralphabet:

Anton	Otto
Ärger	Ökonom
Berta	Paula
Cäsar	Quelle
Charlotte	Richard
Dora	Samuel
Emil	Schule
Friedrich	Theodor
Gustav	Ulrich
Heinrich	Übermut
Ida	Viktor
Julius	Wilhelm
Kaufmann	Xanthippe
Ludwig	Ypsilon
Martha	Zacharias
Nordpol	

6 Und der Text: ...

7 Unterschrift: Wolfgang Halm. Wiederholen Sie bitte?

8 Ist dort das Fernamt?

9 Bitte ein Gespräch nach London MAY 2831 (zwo, acht, drei, eins).

10 Sie können direkt wählen. Die Vorwahl von London ist ...

3 This is London MAY 2831 (two, eight, three, one) Geoffrey Burwell.

4 The address: Wolfgang Halm – I'll spell that: H for Harry, A for Andrew, L for Lucy, M for Mary.

5 The English alphabet for spelling:

Andrew	Nellie
Benjamin	Oliver
Charlie	Peter
David	Queenie
Edward	Robert
Frederick	Sugar
George	Tommy
Harry	Uncle
Isaac	Victor
Jack	William
King	Xmas
Lucy	Yellow
Mary	Zebra

6 And the text: ...

7 Signed: Geoffrey Burwell. Would you repeat it, please?

8 Is that the telephone exchange for trunk calls?

9 I want to put a call through to Munich 22 48 79 (double two, four, eight, seven, nine).

10 You can dial direct. The code number for Munich is ...

11 Bitte ein Gespräch mit persönlicher Voranmeldung für Herrn Geoffrey Burwell.	11 I should like to put through a personal call to Mr. Wolfgang Halm.

Am Telefon | ## On the Telephone

1 (Ich rufe an:) Bitte Herrn Meier.	1 (I ring up): Mr. Meier, please.
2 Verbinden Sie mich bitte mit Herrn Meier.	2 Please give me Mr. Meier.
3 Ich möchte gern Herrn Direktor Müller sprechen.	3 I should like to speak to Director Müller.
4 Wann kann ich ihn am besten erreichen?	4 When is the best time to reach him?
5 Könnten Sie ihm etwas bestellen/ausrichten?	5 Could you give him a message?
6 Oder könnte er vielleicht zurückrufen?	6 Or could he call back perhaps?
7 Wollen Sie meine Nummer notieren?	7 Would you like to make a note of my number?
8 Ich bin den ganzen Tag unter Nummer 26 64 78 zu erreichen.	8 The number 26 64 78 will reach me at any time of the day.
9 (Ich werde angerufen:) Hier Wagner.	9 (I am called up:) Mr. Wagner speaking.
10 Wen wollen Sie sprechen? Herrn Moll?	10 Who do you want to speak to? Mr. Moll?
11 Er kann gerade nicht an den Apparat.	11 He can't come to the phone at the moment.
12 Könnten Sie später noch einmal/nochmal anrufen?	12 Could you ring up again later?
13 Ich kann gern etwas bestellen/ausrichten.	13 Can I take a message?
14 Wie war Ihr Name, bitte?	14 What was your name, please?
15 Einen Moment, bleiben Sie am Apparat, er kommt gerade.	15 One moment, hold the line, he's just coming.

16	Ich gebe Ihnen Herrn Moll, einen Augenblick.	16	I'll give you Mr. Moll, just a moment.
17	Er kommt gleich selbst an den Apparat.	17	He'll be on the line himself in a moment.

Beim Friseur

1 Rasieren, bitte.
2 Schneiden, bitte.
3 Nein, nicht waschen. Sie sind frisch gewaschen.
4 Ziemlich kurz, aber hinten und an den Seiten nicht zuviel weg, bitte!
5 Ohne Scheitel, bitte, alles nach hinten.
6 Waschen, schneiden und legen, bitte.
7 Nur ein wenig nachschneiden, bitte.
8 Sie sehen ja, wie ich es hatte.
9 Bitte ja nicht zu kurz auf der Seite.
10 Ja, ich glaube, so ist es gut.

At the Hairdresser's

1 A shave, please.
2 A haircut, please.
3 No, don't wash my hair. It's been washed recently.
4 Fairly short, but not much off at the back and sides, please.
5 No parting, please, brush it back.
6 Wash, cut and set, please.
7 Just trim the ends, please.
8 You can see how I had it before.
9 Please don't cut it too short at the side.
10 Yes, I think it's all right like that.

In der Apotheke, in der Drogerie

1 Bitte etwas gegen Kopfschmerzen (Magenschmerzen).
2 Etwas gegen Fieber (Grippe), bitte.
3 Bitte ein leichtes Schlafmittel (ein Beruhigungsmittel, Reisetabletten).

At the Chemist's

1 Something for a headache (stomach ache), please.
2 Something for a temperature ('flu'), please.
3 Some mild sleeping pills, (a sedative, some pills for travel sickness), please.

4 Bitte ein leichtes Abführmittel.	4 A mild laxative, please.
5 Bitte etwas gegen Durchfall (Brechdurchfall).	5 Something for diarrhoea (and vomiting).
6 Bitte eine elastische Binde.	6 An elastic bandage, please.
7 Ein Päckchen Hansaplast.	7 A packet of Elastoplast, please.
8 Eine Rolle Leukoplast und Verbandmull.	8 A roll of adhesive plaster and lint.
9 Ich hätte gern eine Sonnenschutzcreme, ein Sonnenöl...	9 I want a suntan cream, suntan oil...
10 eine Sonnenbrille	10 sun glasses
11 eine Zahnbürste, Zahnpasta/Zahncreme	11 tooth brush, tooth paste
12 ein Mundwasser	12 mouth wash,
13 eine desodorierende Seife, einen desodorierenden Stift	13 deodorising soap, deodorant stick
14 einen Hautpuder, einen desodorierenden Puder	14 skin powder, deodorising powder
15 Rasierklingen, eine Rasierseife, ein Rasierwasser	15 razor blades, shaving soap, shaving lotion
16 ein Rasierwasser für die Trockenrasur	16 shaving lotion for a dry shave
17 einen Lippenstift	17 lipstick
18 einen Puder, ein flüssiges Make-up/einen flüssigen Puder	18 powder, liquid make-up
19 eine Nagelschere, eine Nagelfeile, ein Nagelnecessaire	19 nail scissors, nail file, manicure set
20 einen Nagellack, einen Nagellackentferner	20 nail varnish, nail varnish remover
21 eine Wimperntusche	21 mascara
22 ein Shampoo, ein Schampun, Lockenwickel	22 shampoo, hair curlers
23 einen Haarfestiger.	23 hair lacquer.

Beim Arzt

1 Ich möchte mich gern untersuchen lassen.

At the Doctor's

1 I should like to be examined.

2 Ich habe hier Schmerzen.	2 I have got a pain here.
3 Ich möchte sicher sein, daß nichts gebrochen ist.	3 I should like to be certain that nothing is broken.
4 Können Sie mir etwas verschreiben?	4 Can you prescribe something for me?
5 Muß ich irgendwie mit dem Essen vorsichtig sein?	5 Must I be careful what I eat in any way?
6 Darf ich so Auto fahren (baden, Tennis spielen)?	6 May I drive (swim, play tennis) like that?
7 Was kann man dagegen machen?	7 What can be done about it?

Beim Zahnarzt / At the Dentist's

1 Mir ist hier eine Plombe/Füllung herausgebrochen.	1 A filling has broken off here.
2 Ich habe sonst nie etwas mit den Zähnen/an den Zähnen.	2 Apart from that, I never have anything wrong with my teeth.
3 Ich habe hier plötzlich Schmerzen.	3 I suddenly have a pain here.
4 Es tut weh, wenn ich etwas Heißes (Kaltes, Süßes) esse.	4 It hurts when I eat something hot (cold, sweet).
5 Ich glaube, es ist neben der Krone.	5 I think it is next to the crown.
6 Das Zahnfleisch blutet leicht.	6 My gums (tend to) bleed easily.
7 Dieser Zahn/diese Wurzel muß gezogen werden.	7 That tooth/root will have to be pulled out.

Lebenslauf, Familie / Life History, Family

(Es handelt sich um Gesprächssätze, nicht um die stereotypen Formulierungen des schriftlichen Lebenslaufs.)	(The following phrases are taken from conversations, and are not the stereotype clichées to be found in a written curriculum vitae.)
1 Ich bin in München geboren.	1 I was born in Munich.

2	Ich bin auf dem Lande/in der Stadt aufgewachsen.	2	I grew up in the country/in the town.
3	Ich war ein paar Jahre im Internat.	3	I spent a few years at boarding school.
4	Mit 18 habe ich (das) Abitur gemacht.	4	I passed the G. C. E. "A" level at 18. (General Certificate of Education at the Advanced level.)
5	Dann habe ich in München und Berlin studiert.	5	Then I studied at Munich and Berlin.
6	Ich bin auf die Universität/die Uni gegangen.	6	I went to university.
7	Mein Bruder hat an der TH studiert. (sprich: Te-Há)	7	My brother studied at the College of Advanced Technology.
8	Zwischendurch war ich ein Jahr in England.	8	In the meantime I spent a year in England.
9	Ich habe dann noch meinen Doktor gemacht.	9	Then I took a doctorate.
10	Ich habe dann noch promoviert.	10	Then I took my doctor's degree.
11	Meine Frau habe ich in London kennengelernt.	11	I met my wife in London.
12	Ihre Eltern waren ja nicht so ganz einverstanden, aber ...	12	Her parents didn't agree altogether, but ...
13	Ich habe ziemlich jung geheiratet.	13	I married fairly young.
14	Und jetzt sind die Kinder auch schon wieder so groß.	14	And now the children are as tall as me.
15	Wie die Zeit vergeht!	15	How time flies!
16	Meine Älteste will sich an Weihnachten verloben.	16	My eldest daughter wants to get engaged at Christmas.
17	Ich weiß ja nicht ..., sie ist noch sehr jung.	17	I don't know ..., she's still very young.
18	Ich finde, sie sollte erst mal fertigmachen.	18	I think she should finish her education first.
19	Irgendeinen Abschluß sollte sie schon haben.	19	She should have some kind of qualification.

20	Mein Sohn weiß noch nicht genau, was er will.	20	My son doesn't quite know what he wants to do yet.
21	Eine Zeitlang wollte er Lehrer werden.	21	For a time he wanted to be a teacher.
22	Das habe ich ihm ausgeredet.	22	I talked him out of that.
23	Es ist schwierig, er ist so vielseitig begabt.	23	It's difficult, he is gifted in so many ways.
24	Aber es hat ja noch Zeit.	24	But there's still plenty of time.
25	Auf jeden Fall soll er ein Jahr nach Amerika.	25	In any event he's to go to America for a year.
26	Vielleicht kann er ein Stipendium bekommen.	26	Perhaps he can get a scholarship.
27	Meiers erwarten das dritte Kind.	27	Meiers are expecting their third child.
28	Die Kinder sind wirklich gut erzogen.	28	The children are really well brought up.
29	Sie verbieten ihnen nicht zuviel, aber sie lassen ihnen auch nicht alles durchgehen.	29	They don't stop them doing too much, but they don't let them get away with everything.
30	Kinder müssen wissen, wo eine Grenze ist.	30	Children have to know how far they can go.
31	Sie können ruhig frech sein, aber nicht ungezogen.	31	It's all right if they're cheeky, but they mustn't misbehave.
32	Zu brav ist ja auch nichts!	32	I don't want them to be too good, either.
33	Wenn Besuch da ist, produzieren sie sich natürlich gern.	33	When we have guests, of course, they like to show off.
34	Aber richtig aufdringlich sind sie nie.	34	But they're never really a nuisance.

Feste, Glückwünsche, Anteilnahme

Festivals, Congratulations, Condolence

1	Alles Gute zum Neuen Jahr!	1	All the best for the New Year!
2	Prosit Neujahr! (beim Anstoßen)	2	Happy New Year! (clinking glasses)

3 Frohe Ostern/fröhliche Ostern!	3 Happy Easter!
4 Schöne/frohe Feiertage! (an Ostern, Pfingsten, Weihnachten)	4 Have a good holiday! (at Easter, Whitsun, Christmas)
5 Frohe Weihnachten!	5 Merry Christmas!
6 Fröhliche Weihnachten und ein gutes neues Jahr!	6 Merry Christmas and a happy New Year!
7 Meinen herzlichsten Glückwunsch zum Geburtstag!	7 Many happy returns of the day.
8 Herzlichen Glückwunsch zur Verlobung/zur Hochzeit/zum Stammhalter!	8 Congratulations on your engagement/marriage (to a man). I hope you will be happy (to a woman). Congratulations on a son and heir!
9 Mein herzliches Beileid.	9 My sincere sympathy, my condolences.

Freizeit
(vgl. Ferien, Urlaub, S. 53)

Leisure
(cf. Holidays, p. 53)

1 Haben Sie ein Hobby?	1 Have you a hobby?
2 Fotografieren Sie? Machen Sie Dias?	2 Do you take photographs? Do you make slides?
3 Treiben Sie Sport? Treiben Sie Gymnastik?	3 Do you go in for sport? Do you do gymnastics?
4 Gehen Sie gern segeln/tanzen/schwimmen/schifahren/bergsteigen/klettern?	4 Do you like to sail/dance/swim/ski / go for mountain hikes / go mountaineering?
5 Lesen Sie gern? Lesen Sie viel?	5 Do you like reading? Do you read much?
6 Gehen Sie viel ins Theater?	6 Do you go to the theatre much?
7 Sammeln Sie auch Briefmarken?	7 Do you also collect stamps?
8 Sammeln Sie Platten?	8 Do you collect records?
9 Spielen Sie auch selbst? Spielen Sie ein Instrument?	9 Do you play yourself, too? Do you play an instrument?

10 Ich gehe für mein Leben gern ins Kino.	10 I love going to the cinema.
11 Am liebsten ist mir ein guter Western/Krimi.	11 I like a good western/detective film best.
12 Was gibt's denn heute?	12 What's on today then?
13 Wo läuft denn der neue Hitchcock?	13 Where is the new Hitchcock on then?
14 Meinen Sie, für die Oper gibt's noch Karten?	14 Do you think there are any opera tickets left?
15 Sicher ist alles ausverkauft.	15 They're certainly all sold.
16 Vielleicht gibt es noch ein paar teure Plätze.	16 Perhaps there are still a few expensive seats left.
17 Das nächstemal bestellen wir rechtzeitig!	17 Next time we must book in good time.
18 Wer singt denn den Figaro? Und wer dirigiert?	18 Who's singing Figaro then? And who's conducting?
19 Gehen Sie mit ins Konzert? Ich habe Karten.	19 Are you coming with me to the concert? I've got tickets.
20 Karajan dirigiert die Berliner Philharmoniker.	20 Karajan is conducting the Berlin Philharmoniker.
21 Geza Anda spielt das Brahms-d-Moll-Konzert.	21 Geza Anda is playing Brahm's concerto in D-minor.
22 Vorher ist die Es-Dur-Symphonie von Mozart.	22 Before that there's Mozart's symphony in E-flat major.
23 Interessieren Sie sich auch für Kammermusik?	23 Are you also interested in chamber music?
24 Was hören Sie am liebsten im Radio?	24 What do you like listening to best on the radio?
25 Heute abend kommt im 2. Programm ein Hörspiel.	25 This evening there's a play on the 2nd Programme.
26 Vorher ist die Übertragung vom Länderspiel Deutschland–Spanien.	26 Before that the international match Germany versus Spain is being broadcast.
27 Ich höre eigentlich wenig Radio, nur die Nachrichten und den Wetterbericht.	27 Actually I don't listen to the radio much, only the news and the weather forecast.

28	Ich verstehe nicht, wie sich manche Leute den ganzen Tag berieseln lassen.		28	I don't understand how some people can leave it on all day.
29	Mein Bruder könnte gar nicht ohne Radio sein!		29	My brother could never be without a radio.
30	Was halten Sie vom Fernsehen?		30	What do you think of television?
31	Manchmal kommen recht interessante Dinge.		31	Sometimes there are quite interesting things.
32	Vor allem das Studienprogramm/das 3. Programm finde ich sehr gut.		32	I think the Educational Programme/the 3rd Programme is particularly good.
33	Haben Sie neulich die Sendung über Frankreich gesehen?		33	Did you see the programme on France the other day?

Ferien, Urlaub | *Holidays*

1	Wir gehen in Urlaub, wenn die Kinder Ferien haben.		1	We go away when the children have their holidays.
2	Ich möchte nur ausspannen, ich habe es nötig.		2	I only want to relax, I need it.
3	Eine ganze Woche lang (jeden Tag) ausschlafen!		3	Enough sleep (every night) for a whole week.
4	Wir wollen es diesmal gemütlich machen.		4	We want to take it easy this time.
5	Wir haben schon bei einem Reisebüro gebucht.		5	We've already booked with a travel agency.
6	Da braucht man sich um nichts weiter zu kümmern.		6	Then you don't have to bother about anything else.
7	Wir fliegen, da verlieren wir nicht soviel Zeit.		7	We're flying, we don't lose so much time that way.
8	Meine Frau möchte gern etwas sehen.		8	My wife would like to see something.

9 Wir fahren mit dem Auto, dann ist man unten beweglicher. („unten" = südlich; „oben", „droben" = nördlich; „drüben" = östlich oder westlich)

10 Wir haben viel vor in den Ferien.

11 Wir wollen bis nach Sizilien runter.

12 Ich glaube, wir schaffen es in vier Tagen, wenn nichts dazwischenkommt.

13 Das nächstemal wollen wir die Riviera machen.

14 Mein Sohn will mit dem Motorrad nach Griechenland.

15 Er ist recht unternehmungslustig.

16 Wir wollen dieses Jahr wieder campen.

17 Vielleicht kaufen wir sogar einen Wohnwagen.

18 Bisher sind wir immer mit dem Zelt gefahren.

19 Es gibt ja jetzt wirklich herrliche Campingplätze!

20 Und man ist völlig unabhängig von Hotels!

21 Das ist doch kein Urlaub für Ihre Frau, wenn sie sich wieder um alles kümmern muß?

22 Ja, schon, aber mit Kindern ist es einfach ideal!

9 We're going by car, then it's easier to get around over there.

10 We've planned to do a lot in the holidays.

11 We want to go down as far as Sicily.

12 I think we can make it in four days, if nothing holds us up.

13 Next time we want to go to the Riviera.

14 My son wants to go to Greece on his motor-cycle.

15 He's very enterprising.

16 We want to go camping again this year.

17 We may even buy a caravan.

18 Up to now we've always gone with our tent.

19 There are really wonderful camping sites now.

20 And you are completely independent of hotels.

21 But that's not much of a holiday for your wife if she still has to bother about everything.

22 That's right, but with children it's simply ideal.

Auto

1 Bekomme ich als Ausländer eine Zollnummer?

2 Wie lange kann ich mit der Zollnummer fahren?

3 Für die kurze Zeit ist vielleicht ein Leihwagen günstiger.

4 Geht das nach Tagen pauschal oder nach Kilometern?

5 Bitte voll/volltanken.

6 Bitte für 10 Mark.

7 Schauen Sie/sehen Sie bitte das Öl nach.

8 Sehen Sie bitte die Luft nach: vorne 1,2 (eins Komma zwei/eins-zwei), hinten 1,4.

9 Geben Sie mir eine Biluxlampe mit, nur für alle Fälle.

10 Haben Sie Original-Ersatzteile?

11 Können Sie sie besorgen?

12 Gibt es hier keine VW-Werkstätte?

13 Können Sie mir den 20 000er (Kundendienst) machen?

14 Schauen Sie doch bitte mal nach, was da fehlt.

15 Da klappert doch etwas!

16 Das muß noch auf Garantie gehen!

17 Das ist wirklich ein praktischer Wagen.

18 Es geht viel rein, und man sitzt recht bequem.

Car

1 Can I have a customs number as a foreigner?

2 How long can I drive with the customs number?

3 Perhaps a hired car is better for the short time.

4 Do you charge so much per day, or according to mileage?

5 Fill her up, please.

6 For £1, please.

7 Please check the oil.

8 Please check the tyre pressure: 17 at the front, 20 at the back.

9 Please give me an anti-dazzle lamp, just in case.

10 Have you got genuine spares?

11 Can you get hold of them?

12 Isn't there a VW garage here?

13 Can you do the 15,000 mile servicing for me, please?

14 Please have a look what the matter is.

15 There's something rattling.

16 That must still be covered by the guarantee.

17 That really is a practical car.

18 You can get a lot in it, and the seats are comfortable.

19 Im Verbrauch und so ist er sehr sparsam.	19 It's very economical to run.
20 Für das Geld kann man nicht mehr verlangen.	20 You can't expect any more for the price.
21 Das muß man den Franzosen schon lassen: Autos können sie bauen!	21 You have to give it to the French: they know how to make cars.
22 Ehrlich gesagt, ich pflege ihn überhaupt nicht.	22 To be quite honest, I don't clean it at all.
23 Er läuft, das ist die Hauptsache!	23 It goes, that's the main thing.

Unfall

Accident

1 Entschuldigen Sie, ich hatte Sie nicht rechtzeitig gesehen.	1 I'm sorry, I didn't see you in time.
2 Hier sind meine Papiere, wollen Sie sich alles notieren?	2 Here are my documents, do you want to make a note of everything?
3 Ich melde es gleich meiner Versicherung.	3 I'll let my insurance know straight away.
4 Wollen Sie die Polizei holen?	4 Do you want to call the police?
5 Ich glaube, wir können uns so einigen.	5 I think we can settle it between ourselves.
6 Ist ja nur ein kleiner Blechschaden.	6 It's only a little dent.
7 Ist ihnen klar, daß ich hier Vorfahrt habe?	7 Do you realise that it's my right of way here?
8 Geben Sie zu, daß Sie eindeutig schuld sind?	8 Do you admit that you are clearly to blame?
9 Der Herr da hat es doch auch gesehen!	9 The gentleman there saw it as well.
10 Ich habe doch genug Zeugen!	10 I've enough witnesses.
11 Also nein, so etwas ist mir doch noch nicht vorgekommen!	11 I really don't know, nothing like this has ever happened to me before.

12 Sie rasen da wie ein Verrückter, und dann wollen Sie mir auch noch die Schuld geben!	12 You tear along like a madman, and then you try to make out it's my fault.
13 Soll ich die Funkstreife holen?	13 Shall I call the police?
14 Nun regen Sie sich nicht auch noch auf!	14 Now don't you start getting excited as well.
15 Die Polizei wird das schon klären.	15 The police will soon clear the matter up.
16 Ist Ihnen etwas passiert?	16 Has anything happened to you?
17 Sind Sie verletzt?	17 Are you injured?
18 Bitte bleiben Sie ganz ruhig liegen!	18 Lie quite still, please.
19 Bitte rufen Sie schnell das Rote Kreuz!	19 Please call the St. John's ambulance at once.
20 Stehen Sie doch bitte nicht hier herum, Sie behindern doch nur die Sanitäter!	20 Please don't stand around here, you're only holding up the ambulance men.

Reise mit der Bahn   Travelling by Train

1 Welches ist die beste Bahnverbindung nach Madrid?	1 Which is the best rail connection to Madrid?
2 Geht das direkt oder muß ich umsteigen?	2 Is that direct or do I have to change?
3 Wie lange hat man da Aufenthalt?	3 How long is the wait there?
4 Und auf der anderen Strecke hat man sofort Anschluß?	4 And on the other line do I have an immediate connection?
5 Notieren Sie mir bitte Abfahrt und Ankunft.	5 Would you note down for me the times of departure and arrival, please?
6 Geben Sie mir Schlafwagen/Liegewagen.	6 I should like a sleeper/couchette.
7 Geben Sie mir bitte eine Platzkarte.	7 I should like to reserve a seat.

8	Zweimal München einfach, bitte.	8	Two singles to Munich, please.
9	Einmal Stuttgart und zurück.	9	A return to Stuttgart, please.
10	Einmal erster (Klasse) Stuttgart.	10	First class to Stuttgart, please.

Flugreise

Travelling by Air

1	Ich möchte für Sonntag Madrid buchen.	1	I should like to book to Madrid for Sunday.
2	Fliegt Iberia oder Lufthansa?	2	Does Iberia or Lufthansa fly there?
3	Gut, fliegen wir Iberia.	3	Good, let's fly by Iberia.
4	Können Sie den Rückflug auch gleich bestätigen, für den 24.?	4	Can you confirm the return flight too, for the 24th?
5	Ist wirklich alles ausgebucht?	5	Is everything really booked up?
6	Und wie sieht es mit der Warteliste aus?	6	And what about the waiting list?

In der fremden Stadt

In a Strange Town

1	Bitte einen Führer von München, mit Stadtplan.	1	A guide to Munich, please, with a map of the town.
2	Entschuldigen Sie, kennen Sie sich hier aus?	2	Excuse me, do you know your way around here?
3	Ich glaube, ich habe mich verlaufen.	3	I think I've lost my way.
4	Ich möchte zur Alten Pinakothek/zum Bahnhof.	4	I should like to go to the Alte Pinakothek (art gallery)/to the station.
5	Verzeihung, welche Straßenbahn geht zur Oper?	5	Excuse me, which tram goes to the opera house?
6	Fährt der Bus nach Nymphenburg.	6	Does this bus go to Nymphenburg?

7	Wie komme ich am schnellsten zum Flughafen?		7	Which is the quickest way to the airport?
8	Kommen Sie mit? Ich sehe mir den Dom an.		8	Are you coming with me? I'm going to look at the cathedral.
9	Ich gehe in die Oper/in eine Ausstellung.		9	I'm going to the opera / to an exhibition.
10	Ich gehe ins Museum/ ins Theater/ins Kino.		10	I'm going to the museum / to the theatre / to the cinema.
11	Ich möchte nur ein bißchen bummeln.		11	I'd just like to stroll around a bit.
12	Kommen Sie, wir machen einen kleinen Stadtbummel.		12	Come on, let's go for a stroll through the town.
13	Ich bin schon länger hier.		13	I've been here for some time now.
14	Es gefällt mir gut hier.		14	I like it here.
15	Ich habe mich sehr gut eingelebt.		15	I've settled down very well.
16	Sogar ans Klima habe ich mich gewöhnt.		16	I've even got used to the climate.
17	Ich möchte gar nicht mehr weg.		17	I don't want to go away.
18	Ich finde die Stadt schrecklich.		18	I think the town's awful.
19	Ich bin froh, wenn ich wieder zu Haus bin.		19	I'll be glad when I'm back home.
20	Ich möchte nicht für immer hier sein.		20	I shouldn't like to live here for ever.

Polizei, Justiz, Verwaltung

Police, Justice, Administration

1	Muß ich das wirklich alles ausfüllen?		1	Do I really have to fill all that in?
2	Name – Vorname – Geburtsdatum		2	Name – Christian name – date of birth.
3	Geburtsort		3	Place of birth.

4	Familienstand: verh. = verheiratet, led. = ledig, verw. = verwitwet, gesch. = geschieden.	4	Marital status: married, single, widowed, divorced.
5	Staatsangehörigkeit – Reisepaß-Nr.	5	Nationality – Passport No.
6	Beruf – ständiger Wohnsitz.	6	Profession – permanent address.
7	Die Nummer weiß ich leider nicht auswendig.	7	I'm afraid I don't know the number by heart.
8	Ich habe dummerweise meine Papiere im Hotel/im Wagen.	8	How silly of me! I've left my papers in the hotel/car.
9	Ich bin mit dieser Behandlung nicht einverstanden!	9	I object to the way I'm being treated.
10	Es muß alles ein Irrtum sein!	10	It must all be a mistake.
11	Ich werde mich beschweren!	11	I shall complain.
12	Sie verwechseln mich sicher!	12	You must be mixing me up with someone else.
13	Verständigen Sie bitte sofort den englischen Konsul!	13	Please contact the British consul immediately.
14	Ich verlange, daß Sie mich mit dem Konsul sprechen lassen!	14	I insist that you let me speak to the consul.
15	Sie können doch nicht einfach das Auto beschlagnahmen!	15	You can't just confiscate the car.
16	Zuerst haben sie mich auf der Polizei vernommen.	16	First they questioned me at the police station.
17	Sie haben mich für einen lang gesuchten Schmuggler gehalten.	17	They thought I was a smuggler they've been looking for for ages.
18	Beim Untersuchungsrichter hat sich alles aufgeklärt.	18	The magistrate cleared everything up.
19	Inzwischen hatten sie meine Papiere geholt.	19	In the meantime they'd fetched my papers.